Facts About the Wombat

By Lisa Strattin

© 2019 Lisa Strattin

Facts for Kids Picture Books by Lisa Strattin

Little Blue Penguin, Vol 92

Chipmunk, Vol 5

Frilled Lizard, Vol 39

Blue and Gold Macaw, Vol 13

Poison Dart Frogs, Vol 50

Blue Tarantula, Vol 115

African Elephants, Vol 8

Amur Leopard, Vol 89

Sabre Tooth Tiger, Vol 167

Baboon, Vol 174

Sign Up for New Release Emails Here

http://LisaStrattin.com/subscribe-here

Monthly Surprise Box

http://KidCraftsByLisa.com

Contents

INTRODUCTION

The wombat is a medium-sized marsupial that is found only in Australia and the surrounding islands. They are burrowing mammals that spend most of the day underground, coming out at night to eat.

The common wombat is thought to be a descendant of the giant wombat that existed around 50 million years ago. But the Giant Wombat is now extinct, this is thought to be caused by people hunting them and habitat loss. As more people moved to the areas which were their natural habitats, the wombats were pushed out.

CHARACTERISTICS

The wombat is like other marsupials (the kangaroo, for example) in that they have a pouch where their babies stay safe when they are young.

Wombats can be very friendly with people, but this is not always the case. Sometimes they are testy and can hurt you with their claws or by biting.

Their teeth grow continuously, like some other animals, so they need to gnaw on things to keep them ground down to the right size.

APPEARANCE

They have long claws which they use when digging their underground burrows. Wombat burrows can easily become an extensive network of underground tunnels leading to small chambers and are considered a nuisance to agriculture by farmers. Most of them are solitary animals but some have been known to form underground colonies with others.

They also have long pointed ears and fine fur. The common wombats have no hair on the nose, but there are others called the hairy-nosed wombats. The hairy-nosed wombats are silver-gray, but the common wombats vary in color from pale gray to a rich brown. Males and females are similar in appearance.

LIFE STAGES

Like all other marsupials, there is a warm pouch on the female's belly where the wombat babies are nurtured for the first few months of life. When the baby wombats are first born they are very small and crawl into the mother wombat's pouch almost immediately after birth.

The baby wombat stays in the pouch until it is around 5 months old. By the time the baby wombat is roughly 7 months old, it is able to care for itself, leaving the mother, digging tunnels and finding food.

LIFE SPAN

Wombats have been known to live for as long as 25 years in the wild! Some have been observed living much longer in captivity. This is probably because people are taking good care of them and they don't have to worry much about predators.

SIZE

Wombats can grow to be as long as almost 4 feet, and they weigh anywhere from 45 to 78 pounds. They are about as big as a medium- to large-sized dog!

HABITAT

Wombats stay underground in their tunnel system much of the time. They like soil that is loose enough for them to dig into and create the tunnels and compartments where they live. They mostly come out at night when they are looking for food.

DIET

The common wombat is a nocturnal Wombats eat many types of grasses, shoots and bark. They need to keep gnawing on things like tree bark in order to keep their growing teeth at a good size so they can eat well. If the teeth grow too long, the wombat might not be able to close its mouth, and then wouldn't be able to eat!

FRIENDS AND ENEMIES

Wombats have a few natural predators including foxes and dingos. Although the wombat is relatively defenseless when it is roaming around at night, they are generally well protected in their underground burrows as many predators cannot follow the wombat into the narrow, complex tunnels.

SUITABILITY AS PETS

There are people who have successfully kept a wombat as a pet. However, they are not for everyone. They are a pretty good sized animal and with their sharp claws could certainly hurt you.

They might be illegal to have in your area of the world, since they are native to only a few places. It's probably best for you to see if your city's zoo has them and you can see them there.

COLOR ME

COLOR ME

COLOR ME

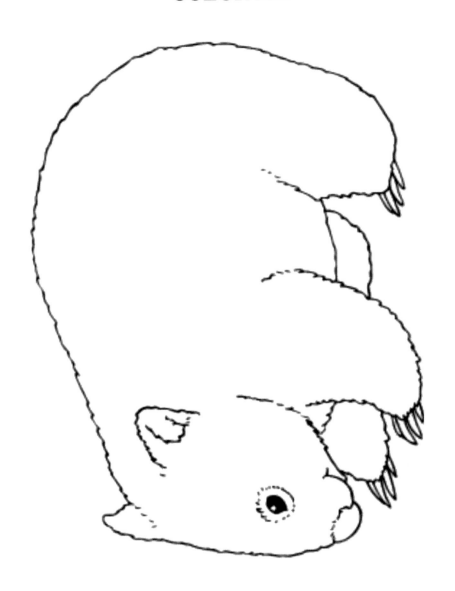

COLOR ME

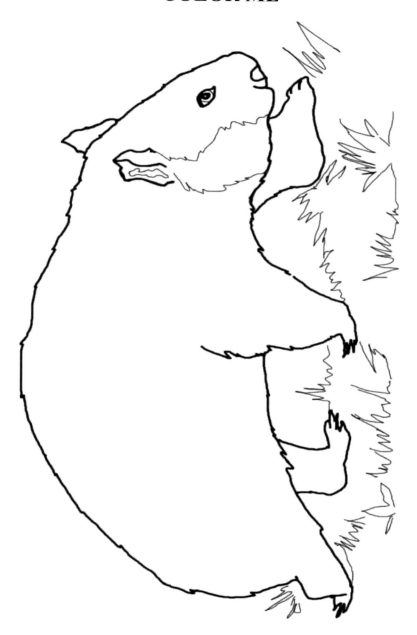

COLOR ME

COLOR ME

COLOR ME

COLOR ME

Please leave me a review here:

http://lisastrattin.com/Review-Vol-203

For more Kindle Downloads Visit Lisa Strattin Author Page on Amazon Author Central

http://amazon.com/author/lisastrattin

To see upcoming titles, visit my website at LisaStrattin.com– all books available on kindle!

http://lisastrattin.com

PLUSH WOMBAT TOY

You can get one by copying and pasting this link into your browser:

http://lisastrattin.com/PlushWombat

MONTHLY SURPRISE BOX

Get yours by copying and pasting this link into your browser

http://KidCraftsByLisa.com

Made in the USA
Middletown, DE
28 September 2019